Dance
Inspiration
Journal & Notebook
with Destiny Wimpye

FOLLOW *Your* DESTINY

Dance Inspiration Journal & Notebook with Destiny Wimpye

Summary: Stunning studio dance poses featuring Destiny Wimpye. Left-side photos with right-side lines for dance corrections, to-do lists, notes, diary entries, gratitude journaling, travel diary, poetry, etc.

Paperback ISBN: 978-1-955555-78-4
Hardcover ISBN: 978-1-955555-79-1

JUVENILE NONFICTION / Language Arts / Journal Writing
JUVENILE NONFICTION / Performing Arts / Dance
LITERARY COLLECTIONS / Diaries & Journals
PERFORMING ARTS / Dance / Choreography & Dance Notation

Discounts available for large-quantity purchases. Contact Once Upon a Dance.

Thank you, Dan Lao of Dan Lao Photography
Cover Photo: Dan Lao | Title Page Photo: Dan Lao | Opposite: Dan Lao

This Journal Belongs to:

_____

Date:

_____

Photo by Dan Lao

Photo by Dan Lao

Photo by Dan Lao

Photo by Dan Lao

Photo by Dan Lao

Photo by Dan Lao

Destiny is a talented dancer, actress and model who hails from Atlanta, Georgia. She moved to Los Angeles in 2013 to train at the Debbie Allen Dance Academy, where she honed her skills in ballet and other dance styles. She has performed with renowned artists such as Mariah Carey, Jill Scott, and Debbie Allen. She's even performed at the White House for the Obama Administration.

Destiny's acting career has also taken off, with appearances in commercials for Toyota, ABCmouse, and Macy's, and roles in TV shows such as *Raven's Home*, *Speechless*, *The Odd Couple*, and *The Wonderful World of Disney: Magical Holiday Celebration*.

Beauty and grace make Destiny a sought-after dancewear and cosmetics model. You'll find her at Discount Dance, All About Dance, and Mariaa Dancewear, and she was featured in a makeup campaign for Hourglass Cosmetics with Twyla Tharp.

Destiny trained at Colburn Dance Academy, Pacific Northwest Ballet School, The Ailey School, School of American Ballet, and Chautauqua Dance Program. After a successful apprenticeship at Pacific Northwest Ballet, she was promoted to corps de ballet in 2023. Destiny was honored to be named one of the "Top 10 Up and Coming Ballerinas to Watch" by *Dance Spirit Magazine*, and has been featured in *Dance Mogul Magazine* and *Dance Informa Magazine*.

To learn more about Destiny and her amazing journey,
    follow @destinywimpye (Instagram),
    or visit www.DestinyWimpye.com.

OTHER BOOKS BY ONCE UPON A DANCE

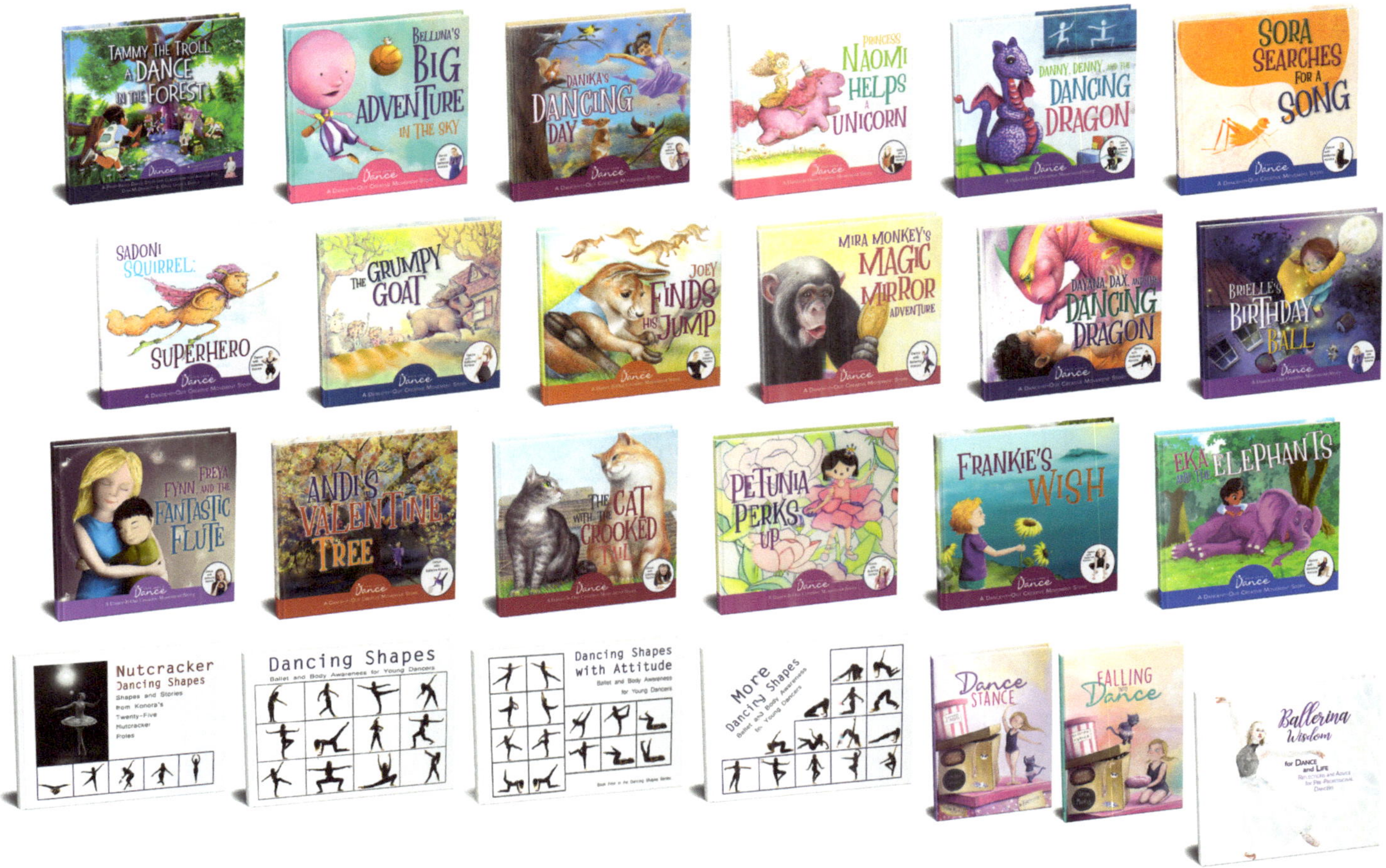

ONCE UPON A Dance

www.ONCE UPON A DANCE.com